Present Tense

Words & Pictures

Present Tense

Words & Pictures

Poems and Photographs from County Mayo
edited by
Macdara Woods and Jim Vaughan

© Mayo County Council

First published in 2006 by Mayo County Council
Áras an Chontae, Castlebar, Co. Mayo

ISBN: 0951962485
Design: Sally O'Leary
Cover Photograph: Glenda Colquhoun
Printed and Bound by Cashin Print, Castlebar

County Arts Office
County Arts Officer: Anne McCarthy
Assistant Arts Officers: Sean Walsh, Ann Marie Lyons

County Library Service
County Librarian: Austin Vaughan

Contents

Réamhrá

Tá áthas mór orm fáilte a chur roimh an bhfoilseachán seo a thugann léiriú breá de Chontae Mhaigh Eo san Aonú Céad is Fiche. Tá an cnuasach seo bailithe le chéile ón bpeirspictíocht is leithne agus áiríonn sé íomhánna ó thíortha eile agus focail i dteangacha eile ag léiriú saibhris agus éagsúlachta Mhaigh Eo.

Ba mhaith liom moladh a thabhairt don Leabharlann Chontae agus do na Seirbhísí Ealaíon Contae ar fhiúntas an fhoilseacháin seo a léiríonn saothar na seirbhísí sin agus a ngealltanais d'fhorbairt chultúir sa Chontae. Is toradh é an leabhar seo ar chomhpháirtíocht thorthúil fhadtéarmach idir an dá sheirbhís, faoi cheannas Austin Vaughan agus Anne McCarthy. Tá tacaíocht leanúnach á fáil ag an Leabharlann agus ag na Seirbhísí Ealaíon ón mBainisteoir Contae, Des Mahon, agus ó na comhaltaí tofa.

Tá an leabhar seo mar thoradh ar phróiseas oscailte soláthraithe a spreag guthanna nua agus íomhánna nua. Is é aidhm an duanaire seo ná filíocht agus grianghrafadóireacht ón gcontae a chur i gcás taispeántais agus ba mhian liom comhghairdeas a dhéanamh leis na heagarthóirí, Macdara Woods agus Jim Vaughan, ar a saothar breá.

Tá súil againn go mbainfidh sibh sult as an leabhar seo agus go ndéanfaidh sibh é a roinnt leo siúd nach bhfuil aithne acu ar Mhaigh Eo mar atá sé inniu. Chomh maith leis na hathraithe uilig a áiríonn muid tá rudaí seasta: áilleacht an tírdhreacha, croíúlacht agus teacht aniar na ndaoine agus an misneach chun síneadh chun tosaigh ar mhaithe le slí nua léirithe a aimsiú.

Gerry Coyle
Cathaoirleach, Comhairle Chontae Mhaigh Eo

vii

Introduction

Poems and photographs are immediate and urgent: they freeze the moment in all its ambiguities. The photograph's immediacy comes from its construction. A moment is cut off from the flow of time by the shutter's action, and by the photographer's intuition and ability to concentrate the scene.

The same compelling immediacy of the initial image also exists for the poet: the subsequent technical problem is to preserve the immediacy throughout the process of writing. The poet edits experience, photographers edit from frozen images and moments.

In calling this book *Present Tense* our intention is to locate the work in its own time and place: increasingly important in our modern world of television, Internet, and everyday international travel, when traditional spatial and temporal dimensions have been so dramatically redrawn.

Some of the images and references in this book are familiar, such as Croagh Patrick, Achill, Westport, Castlebar. They will resonate both with people who have stood in these places and with those who have not. But we have also included burial towers in Iran, railroads in Kosovo, kitchens in Brazil, alongside Sweeney in Erris, the Mayo Rose, and arm-wrestling in Geesala. Just as we have poems in Irish, English, Polish and German: reflecting, we hope, the multiplicities of current reality.

Many of the poets in this book are very well known indeed, and just as many of the photographers have widely appeared in print, while for quite a number of others this is their first publication ever. We feel the picture of the County presented is truer as a result.

But we don't for a moment claim this as the definitive expression of the County. In our inclusions and exclusions we have endeavoured to present the best anthology from the work received. The act of trying to be representative involves leaving some material out.

With this in mind we would like to thank everyone who sent us work, whether it is included in this volume or not. They have all added to the book as it stands, just as they add to the generous measure of the County – as timeless and ongoing as the present tense itself.

Macdara Woods   Jim Vaughan

Acknowledgements

Mayo County Council wish to acknowledge the contribution of the following:

Ger Reidy & Terry McDonagh

Verlag Kiepenheuer & Witsch, Köln

Anna Galt & Ewa Sadowska

Special thanks to the editors Macdara Woods & Jim Vaughan

Ein Jahr
Für Heidi die bei ihm war (1982)

Heinrich Böll

Ein Jahr
Für Heidi die bei ihm war (1982)

Ein jahr hat keine Zeit
Rai
ist keine
heilt nicht
was da verstreicht
zwischen Achill + Arlesheim
zwischen Merten Metternich
Kelz und Langenbroich
wo die Äpfel Äpfel Äpfel reifen
während Du lagst
in Unterlegenhardt
und gewußt gelitten gelitten hast
der Abschied vom Hörnli
ein Grab am Bromhübel
die Bäume wurden herbstlich
und winterkahl
graues Gehänge über Köln
Giftwolken über Wesseling
Krähen am blassen Himmel
in Kelz die Judengräber im Schnee
pompöses Dauernichts
der Gipfel

A Year
For Heidi who was with him (1982)

A year has no time/Rai/Is not/Does not heal/What has passed there/Between Achill and Arlesheim/Between Merten Metternich/Kelz and Langenbroich/Where the apples apples apples ripen/While you lay/In Unterlegenhardt/And knowingly suffered had suffered/The farewell from the Hörnli/A grave at the Bromhübel/The trees became autumnal/And winter bare/Greyness hangs above Cologne/Poison clouds above Wesseling/Crows in the pale sky/In Kelz the Jewish graves in the snow/Pompous eternal nothingness/The peak

1

Deine hinterlassenschaft
Licht
verkörpertes Licht
gelitten gewußt gelitten
Die Ruhe der Brunnen
Brachmettstraße
Steine Häuser Formen
in Hochwald
Kaffees
im Rössli im Ochsen
Dornering Chemei Schönmatt
Dorneck und unter den Bäumen
auf der Terrasse in Dornach
Tage des Terrors in Brünn
das Blut an Deiner treuen Hand
und die Ewigkeit der Wartestunden
da bei Nikolsburg
Schillerstraße
Belvederestraße
Hülchratherstraße
mit Hammer und Meißel
am Kölner Dom
oh Chlodwigplatz
Jahre in Keel und Dugort
die Steine im Gras bei den Kühen
Aus der Zeit gefallen Dein Tisch
die Bäume wurden grün
und blühten

/Your legacy/Light/Embodied light/Suffered knowingly suffered/The peace of the well/Brachmettstraße/Stones shapes houses/In Hochwald/Coffees/In the Rössli in the Ochsen/Dornering Chemei Schönmatt/Dorneck and under the trees/On the terrace in Dornach/Days of terror in Brühn/Blood on your faithful hand/And the eternity of hours waiting/There by Nikolsburg/Schillerstraße/Belevederestraße/Hülchratherstraße/With hammer and chisel/At Cologne cathedral/Oh Chlodwigplatz/Years in Keel and Dugort/The stones in the grass by the cows/Fallen out of time your table/The trees became green/And bloomed/

schlimm Rai schlimm

woe es am schönsten ist

schlimm

verfallen Rai Deine Weiderechte

in Bellanasally und Orghnadirka

die Fischrechte an den Klippen

von Carricknagellinagubloo

und wieder auf Gipfeln grünend

Raketenhaine verkünden das Nichts

In Langenbroich

erkunden die Eichelhäher

den Stand der Kirschernte

oh Rai

Zwischen Merten Metternich

Kelz und Langenbroich

beginnt das Jahr

hat keine Zeit

ist keine

heilt nicht

was da verstreichen wird

sieh Deine Brüder Rai

auch den Bruder

der Dir vorausging

sieh Deine Mutter

mich

und Heidi

die immer bei Dir war

Terrible Rai terrible/Where it is most beautiful/Terrible/Expired Rai your grazing rights/In Bellanasally and Orghnadirka/Your fishing rights at the cliffs/Of Carricknagellinagubloo/And again on greening mountain tops/Rocket groves proclaim the void/In Langenbroich/The jaybirds investigate/The progress of the cherry harvest/Oh Rai/Between Merten Metternich/Kelz and Langenbroich/The year begins/Has no time/Is not/Does not heal/What passes there/See your brothers Rai/Also the brother /Who went before you/See your mother /Me /And Heidi/Who was always with you.

Lily

Dragonfly II Daffodils

Wild Flowers

Bringing Home A Rose

Lily

Michael Gannon

6

Dobromir Petrov

Daffodils

Dobromir Petrov

Thomas Reaney

8

Art Ó Súilleabháin

Night Road

The Second Night

Sweeney In Erris

The Dawn Chorus

Cabinet

Salvation

This Is Not Missing

Kevin Bowen

Night Road

There is a way you forget
the darkness
the way it creeps up
on you on a road
at night

a way you forget
how lonely a light on a hill can be,
or how your own shadow
will startle you when it appears
in the mist

a way you even forget
that hard rush the water makes
as it moves through the ditch
after the rain has pounded
the mountain all day.

There is a way you forget
all this, then you walk out
onto the road one night
and know your life
is nothing without it.

The Second Night

Outside the white cottage, a half-dozen chairs set out.
A run of rocky fields washed in starlight.

Full moon rising off the cliffs
cutting a path to the islands.

Inside the cottage, sounds of children
quieting themselves.

The slow scrape and rattle of chairs
dragged across a linoleum floor.

Last stir of footsteps fading softly
down a darkened road.

A face pressed against glass
stealing a last look out a window.

One night ending.
A second night begins.

Seán Lysaght

Sweeney In Erris

Sweeney sang in a grove of pines
as light skidded off a rippled pool.

A river lost its sweetness seawards.
Oak-leaves gathered on rainy cobbles

where an empire had passed.
Already too late, he sang through the surf

of a windy wood.
Antiquity had been here once. She wrote:

sea-trout running every summer,
loaded with stars.

But light and water took them
to be the ghosts of their glen

in the otherworld of a river,
the raven lording.

Now the place allowed only a linnet
in the company of thistles.

One rowan couldn't redeem
and was too much to condemn,

rhododendron too deeply rooted
in its own bitter shadow

for anyone to bother. Thistledown
flaked from Sweeney's bill

and swept away to a vastness

The Dawn Chorus

Sweeney wasn't the only one to be turned into a bird.
Up there in the cells of branches he met
others who had flown off like him,
leaving their shoes after them in mud.

During his time among the lifers
he heard stories from their roost:
people killed in cold blood,
great harms done to childhood.

But at dawn it was different.
The place rang when the orchestra rehearsed
and Sweeney sang along with the rest
as though his life depended on it.

Una Leavy

Cabinet

She always wanted a china cabinet, polished, triangular
for standing in the corner. It would be grand
for her few precious things —
the swan-shaped butter-dish of orange glass,
the fine bone-china used on Christmas Eve,
gold-banded, fragile wide translucent cups.
Drink up, she'd say, *before the tea gets cold*.

And it was cold
the day we laid her fine white bones
in polished oak,
smothered in tears and stones.

Bríd Quinn

Salvation

My mother and I worked the sticky brown clay.
Mixed it with soft strong compost,
planted first daffodil then crocus and iris.
I asking how, she quietly instructing
more here, less there
heads close together over the fresh earth.

Next morning I see the brown patch among the green,
a fine October mist tending the grave.
In spring spectres of pale yellow
will serve as reminders of life.

Lizann Gorman

This Is Not Missing

I should be leaving you to the pub now
After all it's Tuesday night.
You should be finding it hard to get out of the car
And giving orders about collecting you.

You'll forget your stick and have to come back.

On Thursday I should be picking you up
After you've been to the post office for the pension,
You'd have had two pints in the pub and
Bought the mutton for the week.

You'd be waiting for me in the car park.

You'd have the money in the top pocket of your jacket,
Eventually I stopped arguing with you about it.
Last winter I found you reluctantly plugging in the heater.
I'm entitled as the next to keep myself warm you said.

I miss you more than the things we did together.

St Brendan's

Geesala

Changing Room

Croagh Patrick

St Brendan's

Keith Heneghan

Michael Mc Laughlin

Changing Room

Michael Mc Laughlin

Croagh Patrick

Keith Heneghan

From Cill Aodain To Killeenin

A New Language
Later

Cómharthaí

Gan Deis Acu Athlonnú

Tiger The Cat - MS Diagnosis

Terry McDonagh

From Cill Aodain To Killeenin

Mise Raifteirí an file: I am Raftery the poet.
No house. Nothing, but the hearthstone remains.
A whitethorn has become Raftery's bush. *Child,*
run and tell your teacher before the flame dies.

Old and young recited Cill Aodain
between decades, on their knees,
to lessen the nausea of weak faith
or the strut of a red-eyed schoolmaster.

His name is there: Anthony Raftery
in The Poet's Graveyard in County Galway.
Years ago, my father planted saplings from
Cill Aodain in Craughwell and a small group sang

to the vision of the blind bard. They were
respectful, as if waiting for tales of
his withered eyes, Taffe's horse, Mary Hynes
or even a love song to fill in the long scar from

his hearthstone in Cill Aodain
to his gravestone in Killeenin.

A New Language Later

I began a new language later, and
still don't know a second word for
spate, spoke or the depth of a shadow.

I see people check ties and teeth
in a job agency window. They face
the same words at every interview;
never their own.

Moses heard voices out of
a burning bush. When my friend
heard them, he was committed.

I often talked to myself as a child,
found words in fields and furrows,
made sense of croaking ponds and
answered back – I never had to learn.

Words came, wild as weeds would
or as little threatened trees do, all windy
and quaking. When I fell into water
screaming, I was understood – even
our old dog raised a dog-eye at my cry.

I've also lain stranded between lips
with nothing to say. It's true.

Colette Nic Aodha

Cómharthaí

Ar phríomhbóthar Chamden
díoltar púicíní draíochta,
piocann fear déirce
toitín suas ón gcosán
is caitheann sé é.

Fiche punt ar naoi n-unsa
de phúicíní draíochta ón Cholóim
nó ón Ghuine Mheanchriosach.
Dath rastaiféarach ar luaithreadán,
boscaí beaga nó píopa do ráithneach,

rudaí a bhíonn ag teastáil
ó dhaoine nach bhfuil
chomh sean liom féin,
feicim clóca m'óige
thíos fúm ar an mbóthar.

Ardaíonn an ghaoth,
séidtear duilleoga im éadan,
ní féidir mo shlí abhaile
a aimsiú tríd an smionagar.

Gan Deis Acu Athlonnú

Is laindéir lasta ag an samhradh
an aiteann atá ar dhá thaobh an bhóithrín,
féar gan slacht sa lár,
cuimlíonn sé focharráiste an ghluaisteáin,
osclaíonn geata mar a bheadh méanfach ann.

Gan rian dá laghad de Thí Seoighe le feiceáil,
oiread is cúpla cloch caite ar leathtaobh,
ar nós gur shlog an portach an teach ina hiomlán,
ag goid aon dheis
a bheadh ag an teighleach athlonnú.

Béal dorais tá cúirt leadóige
in áit seanchlós mo mháthair mór.
Gach crann giúise imithe
labhrais ina n-áiteanna,
gan bheith in inmhe fós feadaíl sa ghaoth.

San úllord fia úlla amháin a fhásann,
cró na gcearc, gan oiread is cleiteach
le feiceáil ann, i bhfolach
taobh thiar d'áirse caschoille.
Is taibhse an gáirdín tachtaithe le neantóga.

Jean Tuomey

Tiger The Cat - MS Diagnosis

It jumped unexpectedly
claws digging in, hanging on
not for its sake but to prove its point.
It's in control.

I pretend all is well.
I'm not afraid, I say.
It is tiger not cat size.

I'm not afraid, I repeat,
as I try to detach
the creature from my arms.

Westport Horse Fair From The Fairgreen

Keernaun Sunrise

Michael Varley's Field

Sheep

Hay

Turf

Westport Horse Fair From The Fairgreen

Graham Temple

Keernaun Sunrise

Michael Blake

Michael Varley's Field

Michael Blake

Sheep

Margo McNulty

37

Hay

Olivia Smyth

Turf

Olivia Smyth

Ireland
October 4th 2005

Siopa Oxfam, Caisleán An Bharraigh

Dealbh Naomh Antaine

The Village Bakery

Newport 2000 – 2004

My Dad

Tassels Of Trust

Mundanimity

John Corless

Ireland – October 4th 2005

Today on the news they were on about money again.
Money wasted on a computer for the Health Service.
A hundred and fifty million they said.
Some expert said it was a hundred and seventy.
Million.
Money wasted.
It's not wasted they said, we have the computers.
So it's not wasted.
It's not wasted.
We have the computers.

Today on the news they were on about money again.
Sometimes they can't get through.
Can't get an answer on the phone.
The women.
On the helpline – they can't get an answer.
There isn't enough staff to answer the phone.
So they'll have to wait.
Wait for another while.
Wait for an answer, wait for help.
Wait in the fear and the violence.
Wait for an answer.

We have the computers but no one to answer.

Caitríona Uí Oistín

Siopa Oxfam, Caisleán An Bharraigh

Boladh na háite is mó a shásaíodh í, boladh daoine,
Cumhra an tsaoil a caitheadh cheana, a bhí á thairscint arís;
Théadh sí timpeall ag méardrú gach uile rud,
Á mbreatnú go grinn, aoibh ainglí fána béal aici.
I ndiaidh am lóin is mó ba gnách léi dul thart,
An uair bheannaithe úd idir a dó agus a trí,
Bhíodh an t-urlár gona chuid ráillí nach mór fúithi féin.

Thógadh gach uile bheilt *diamante*, scrúdaíodh na blúsanna,
Na sciortaí fada, na géinte gorma ró-rite, na *halter-necks*.
Bhaineadh an uile bhróg amach as na boscaí,
B'aoibhinn go deo léi na cuaráin síoda oíche a bhíodh ann,
A neamhchéillí is a bhí said, míorúilt strapaí agus aeir;
Agus na hataí, féastaí tuí agus ribíní agus bláthanna beaga sróil,
Ba ghleoite léi iadsan, thar aon ní eile.

Seanaithne ag na mná freastail uirthi faoin am seo,
Bheannaíodh go cneasta di ar a bealach amach,
Ise agus iadsan, ansin i measc na gcarad ar feadh tamaill,
Ar oilithreacht i ndomhan na gcuimhní athláimhe.

Dealbh Naomh Antaine

Cén scéal agat a dhuine?
'Is trom babaí i bhfad' a deir tú,
Tú ansin is d'ualach áthais id' bhaclainn agat.
Agus is troimde do chroí an carn mór scéalta,
Chuile mhac máthar agus a scéal féin aige,
Chuile bhean ag brú an cháis roimpi, in éineacht leis na pingneachaí.
Éisteann tú, ní athraíonn do dhreach chiúin chalma.
Dearbhaíonn a nguí, admhaíonn a bpian, fóireann orthu,
Is féidir leatsa é a sheasacht, is chuige sin atá tú.

Níl ann ach aon ní amháin a chriogann thú,
A dhéanann ualach ceart de d'ualach.
An fear óg dubh-ghléasta sin a thagann in am marbh na hoíche,
Nach n-abrann aon ní, nach n-amharcann ort;
Nuair a mhúchann seisean soilsí an tséipéil, pléascann do chroí ar fad,
An leanbh féin id' bhaclainn, caoineann.

Mary Whelan

The Village Bakery, Newport
2000 – 2004

They gave us bread
for three good years,
and summer fruits,
and Christmas smells
that wafted through the town.

In summer, tourists filled
the tables on the steps,
and fed the dog
and bought the cakes
for evenings
out in Achill and Corraun.

And when winter came
I loved
to warm my hands on
mugs of tea,
and breakfast with the staff
when things were quiet.

The Bakery,
a sign that all was well,
that bread was blessed
and shared,
has closed,
and I am desolate.

Bríd Conroy

My Dad

Belongings in paper bags
Tied tightly in orange string
Adventure to offer
No phone numbers to give

Women lined the streets
To watch those men
Driving, speeding through Europe,
War just gone

They came back to Parnell Square
To dances, to wives
To me, to street lights,
I am glad he came, my Dad

Maureen Maguire

Tassels Of Trust

She was the lily of the valley in the morning
She was the cup of cocoa at night
She was the shout for dinner at one
She was the smell of freshly baked bread
She was the gramophone in the midst of tears
She was the laughter in the Hollow Bog
She was the spinner of wool on a winter's day
She was the storybook on a Sunday afternoon
She was the prayer at the blessed well
She was the primroses in the jam jar in May
She was the berry on the sprig of holly at Christmas
She was the plate of beestings after the cow calved
She was the bleached blankets spread out in Shrah Fullach
She was the washing drying on the yellow whin
She was the reason we made tea in the sugar bowl
She was the reason we had boiled sweets on fair day
She was the clappers after the churning
She was the herrings on the tongs
She was the fresh bowl of raspberries
She was the blackberry pie for lunch by the river
She was the melody in the wind that skimmed the waves
She was my fountain of knowledge
She was the reason I stayed
She was the reason I didn't want to leave
She was my grandmother

Benny Martin

Mundanimity

I am the doer of the mundane tasks,
The tender of the tribal fire,
Picker up of tripsome things;
The adder of small figures;
And hander-on of totals.
The thinker of the small thoughts
That never see the light of day,
The occupant of small life space,
Unhurried in a hurried world
The sleeper of the night sleep.

Mulranny Golf Links

Pontoon *For Your Convenience*

Bog Holes, North Mayo

Ball Alley I, II, III

Found Negative

House And River

Mulranny Golf Links

Jan Pesch

For Your Convenience

Paul Fullard

Pontoon (with kind permission
of Dr. John F Connolly)

Paul Fullard

51

Bog Holes, North Mayo

Jan Pesch

53

Andrew Hebden

Found Negative

Paul Tarpey

House And River

Dobromir Petrov

Slievemore: The Abandoned Village

Messages To The Wind

Portal

Hailing The Oystercatcher, Dooega, Achill

Leaving Go

Etruscan   Goats Climb The Divide

Hospitality

Comfort

John F Deane

Slievemore: The Abandoned Village

You park your car on the low slope
    under the graveyard wall. Always
there is a mound of fresh-turned earth, flowers
    in pottery vases. There is light, from the sea and the wide
western sky, the Atlantic's
    soft-shoe nonchalance, whistle
of kestrels from the lifting mists, furze-scents, ferns, shiverings –
    till suddenly you are aware
you have come from an inland drift of dailiness to this shock
    of island, the hugeness of its beauty
dismaying you again to consciousness. Here
    is the wind-swept, ravenous
mountainside of grief; this is the long tilted valley where famine
    came like an old and infamous flood
from the afflicting hand of God. Beyond all
    understanding. Inarticulate. And pleading.
Deserted. Of all but the wall-stones and grasses,
    humped field-rocks and lazy-beds; what was commerce and family
become passive and inert, space
    for the study of the metaphysics of humanness. You climb
grudgingly, aware of the gnawing hungers,
    how the light leans affably, the way an urchin once might have watched
from a doorway;
    you are no more than a dust-mote on the mountainside,
allowing God his spaces; you are

watercress and sorrel, one with the praying of villagers,
one with their silence, your hands
    clenched in overcoat pockets, standing between one world
and another.
    It has been easier to kneel
among the artefacts in the island graveyard, this harnessing of craft
    to contain our griefs;
here, among these wind-swept, ravenous acres
    where we abandon our acceptably deceased to the mountain earth.
In grace. In trustfulness.
    This, too, the afflicting hand of God. Beyond all
understanding. Inarticulate. Though in praise.

Messages To The Wind
Keem Bay, Achill Island

You come stumbling, stranger, into a world too great
for your littleness; rocks off-shore, the ocean
breaking, and further out what could be tips of old
mountains, breaching, like hump-back sharks

basking; storms off the Atlantic have laid the telegraph poles
over on their sides, like slanted sailors, flinging messages
to the winds; mid-day and in the azure sky
the moon is thin as a haw upon a window-pane;

backwash of the world, salt secret and backward
sand-beach; and there she is, old lady dressed in black, asleep
in the deck-chair, her grey hair fondled by the breeze,
sea-water already reaching for her shoes, and, scattered

mullion everywhere: sailors by-the-wind, beyond-the-blue-sky
blue, their shivering; the earth, stranger, gentling
at your feet, its mythic scope and sanctity yet you
gaze only inwards with the mien of a hurt god.

Colette Nic Aodha

Portal

Winter Atlantic water making small white birds of itself
as it strolls towards the shore in a piecemeal fashion. I thought the whites alive at first,
wondered where this colony hailed from,

they stretched from Murrisk Head right across Clew Bay.
A streak on the pane places a flag on the summit of the bump
that rests between two Nephins. Black wispy clouds try to veil

lumps of snowy sunshine but fail to stop sea-mountain illumination.
Not even the most adept painter could transfer such velvet shadows and brown
mountain light that warms my eyes; the crushed multi-blue silk of the ocean,

pagan god emerging through cloud above Croagh Patrick, gothic cattle revering grass,
hilly bramble-stitched right-of-ways, walks to the strand,
distant houses that are pearls strung at the feet of hills.

Wagtail hopping on the pavement outside taps out hunger. Bright and dark cloud
worlds collide, a rainbow forms beneath them;
orange aflame, red edging, yellow sandwiched between green and indigo,

no extending arc, just bare essentials. Not of this world. I want to search
for a forgotten people where the rainbow sinks into the foothills. As I lift my eyes
from the page I notice all has disappeared, even the clouds.

Ancient rocks that wouldn't be moved are whispering something to its place of
sacrifice on the mountain, breeze carries secrets into every curve of the bay.
Here the elements are the only gods.

Mark F Chaddock

Hailing The Oystercatcher, Dooega, Achill

Yesterday,
out among blue-black rocks and oystercatcher cries
I sketched the wind.

Finishing up
in that calm euphoria descends
when an image declares more than the placed marks,
a stranger behind me quipped,
It must be a fine thing to pluck something out the air,
Out of time.

We had things in common; nature; art; old Ireland.
I pointed along the shoreline,
That black and white bird probing the mud; the oystercatcher, the sea-pie.
What's the Irish for that?

He went back into himself,
as a boy under ever-blue skies and rock-flung spray,
fishing off the rocks for mackerel and coley,
air filled with piping and birds' wings.
Until he caught the word smiling, spoke it shyly, with affection.

Something familiar in the soft sounds,
like a summons of the bird's spirit, ancient and wise;
a language of poets as the everyday.

And I longed to swim in that ocean he fished as a youth.
To make it real and familiar.
To wear it proudly, close to my heart like a medal.
To pluck Irish words out the air, haul them sparkling out of time.
To hail the oystercatcher, by her native name.

J. McCormick Phillips

Leaving Go

The beach lies far behind
where we built all those castles
a plastic-spaded mother
shaping dreams from moulds.

Now I watch from ramparts
through wild pennant hair
as you escape the harbour
in your jaunty boat:

Sails filling, grey seas.

Sabra Loomis

Etruscan

Rain is coming,
bringing cattle
home through the hedges at nightfall.

Hurry to the gate –
to look beyond, to see beyond
ourselves: through a web of roots
uphill, through a gap in the willows.

Wild waters beyond childhood
breathe into the dusk.
They are carried like weight into tree-bark,
and the listening hide of trees.

Forage for the spells
that lie underneath a gate.

Bringing cattle to the edges of fields;
to push their heads forward
and drink beneath the wires.

They breathe in the dusk
behind a field-gate,
with wide, Etruscan eyes
and with a ragged breath, at nightfall.

Goats Climb The Divide

They were sewing,
butting their heads through canvas
to sew the maroon and green heather,
the bright canvas waves.

I liked the way they climbed
into the rough sky above hills
with ribbed houses of coral –
the blue and white shreds
of beaded clouds.

The goats looked down at me once,
curling their way over hills.
They were walking through the oval night.

They worked their way under the wire
then out, through a torn, iron gate.

They climbed the nervous corners
of the divide, to go on upward.
Keeping the outline of a path
through rough seas of heather;
finding a foothold in bare rock.

I liked the way the goats
climbed the divide of hills.
They were singing in their hides
to sew the few, bright curves of heather,
the maroon and green waves.

Ursula Kelly

Hospitality

Your only companion
Is the perfect curve
Of yourself
Mirrored
Upside down
In the still January water

And I swear that you watch me
Recede from you

I want to cry
For the lone swan
In cold flood waters
Waiting for death
Or another passing flock
Who may break their formation
To allow a stranger
In

Comfort

Like the slow showers of May
That permeate the soil's parched crust
I long for your unknown touch
To heal me
With the uncertainty
Of opposites
Recognising
The mystery
Of chance encounter

Pilgrim

Feet Of The Pilgrim

Golden Rosary

Untitled I & II

President Visits Westport July 2001

The Sawdoctors At Castlebar

Michael Mc Laughlin

Feet Of The Pilgrim

Michael Mc Laughlin

Golden Rosary

Michael Mc Laughlin

Untitled I

Andrew Hebden

Untitled II

Andrew Hebden

President Visits
Westport July 2001

Conor Mc Keown

77

The Sawdoctors At Castlebar

Graham Temple

The First Time I Met The Blues (after Buddy Guy)

Light

Saturday Night's Social Scene

A Midsummer's Night Scene

Cúl Mo Chinn

Bouquet

Crows At Cappagh

The Medicine I Dressed Up In

Painting The Blue Sky Black

Ger Reidy

The First Time I Met The Blues
(after Buddy Guy)

The first time I met the Blues
I was sittin' beside Kathleen,
yeah, the first time I met the Blues
I was sittin' beside Kathleen,
when the master stroked her thigh.

Yeah, we cried, c'mon everybody.

Ballinasloe for shoes,
Tuam for sugar,
Ballinasloe for shoes,
Tuam for sugar,
Newbridge for ropes.

The next time I met the Blues
her hair was glued with tears,
yeah the next time I met the Blues
her hair was glued with tears,
her head ringing from a blow on the ears.

Yeah, we cried, c'mon everybody.

MacDonagh and MacBride,
and Connolly and Pearse,
MacDonagh and MacBride,
and Connolly and Pearse,
a terrible beauty is born.

The last time I met the Blues,
yeah, she was a-swingin',
the last time I met the Blues
I saw her in the hayshed swingin',
yeah, her husband he found her a-swayin'.

Yeah, we cried, everybody.

Light

I stood unsure on broken toys
and grabbed its first sunrays on a May morning,
ran to the top of our hill to gaze in awe
at the colour of cumulus towers over the bay.

On frosty nights I saw it reflect
off oily pools outside Marconi's chip shop,
spied it resting in cathedral pews mid-afternoon,
listened to the silence, absolving.

I felt the first terminal sadness after school
as it crawled up the floral wallpaper,
watched it trickle through the bicycle shed
over the pandemonium of old furniture – soothing.

I glimpsed lovers abandoned in moon meadows
as it angled its way towards me in a ruined cottage,
waited as it crept upon a laddered stocking
while Michael Dillon announced cattle prices from Tuam.

But I never knew what it was for until one evening
a watery sun peeked out between huge clouds,
its last rays through the cracked bathroom window
discovering your naked profile – looking away.

Peggy McGing

Saturday Night's Social Scene

At half past ten the clock has struck,
the lights are dim and frost is in the air.
Slowly traffic moves up and down the street,
across the way, not far from the corner shop,
two young lovers meet.

In the shadow of the half-light street
and around the corner, people walk
making their way to music-pubs and bars.
Taxis pass by with yellow signs on top.

It is half past ten on this winter night
of Saturday's social scene.

Mary Catherine Reilly

A Midsummer's Night Scene

Watch Titania
Sweep into the room
With a gossamer gown
Beaded, laced and spun
By a spider seamstress
On a tiny spinning wheel.
Crying all the time
For Oberon.
How could I have got it so wrong?

Teresa Lally

Cúl Mo Chinn

Aréir is mé im' chodhladh
bhí fhios agam go maith
go raibh bean eile ann,
is cé go rabhas scanraithe
d'eiríos óm leaba
is chuartaíos gach seomra.
Nuair d'fhéachas isteach
sa *mboxroom*, céard d'fheicfinn
ach *device* leagtha leis an bhfalla
'cúl mo chinn.

Bouquet

It was all that, and more.
Of course there was the fatal flaw,
the unthrown bouquet.

How they'd waited and waited.

So the next day
they gathered together
all the bruised
half-broken and
hurt little button-holes

and made as best they could
a bouquet of sorts

and had her stand far away
in the middle of the room.

Catch, catch they cried
and clapped and cheered
when she did.
They were that kind of family,
generous to a fault.
And everyone loves a Bride.

Crows At Cappagh

I should be grateful
it's an airy hospital.
One with patio doors.

Another hot May.
The pines have grown like the prices.

And crows gather with caw-caw tales
of how wonderful it is to flock out here in Cappagh
where free hips,
not to mention wings
are in endless supply;
how they never lose their entitlements.

All the loud-long day I hear them caw
about how great their own young ones
(and also the fathers) are doing
both here and abroad.

And one in particular, Jason,
enters the theatre
perched on the surgeon's
– (the self-same one, gold-toothed!) –
left shoulder;
will peck his eyes out at any hint of jargon.

And no
they don't remember us from other times,
or should they.

Daniel Hickey

The Medicine I Dressed Up In

The medicine I dressed up in was
The pendulum of mind: mood
Itched my skin like slipping vinyl from a groove.

I approached diagnosis with
A gradual, sad astonishment.
And not understanding the argument I

Wept at X-rays on the wall &
At the conclusions of opinion &,
Fingers shivering, dreading the call —

Painting The Blue Sky Black

By Christ I'd long had the notion
Of calculating that ragged distance between self & object,
Of marking out on a measuring-tape uncoiled,
And filming then that forever unfinished scene –
Old Vincent Van Gogh alone in a field,
Scattering vague light on the void.

Like telescope clarity picking stars from night
I pulled focus directly into line of sight.

But though the tumbling sun dropped orange,
  And teased breathing greens from the grass,
    Van Gogh, he just sat at his canvas,
      Painting the blue sky black.

Lost in Seoul I & II

Mud Brick House, Esfahan, Iran

Sky Burial Preparation Halls, Mid-Iran

Railroad

Face

Prayer House, Kosovo

Tree

Francis Van Maele

Lost in Seoul I & II

Mud Brick House, Esfahan, Iran

Michael Conlon

Sky Burial Preparation Halls, Mid-Iran

Michael Conlon

Noreen Hopkins

Prayer House, Kosovo

Noreen Hopkins

Tree

Brendan Derrig

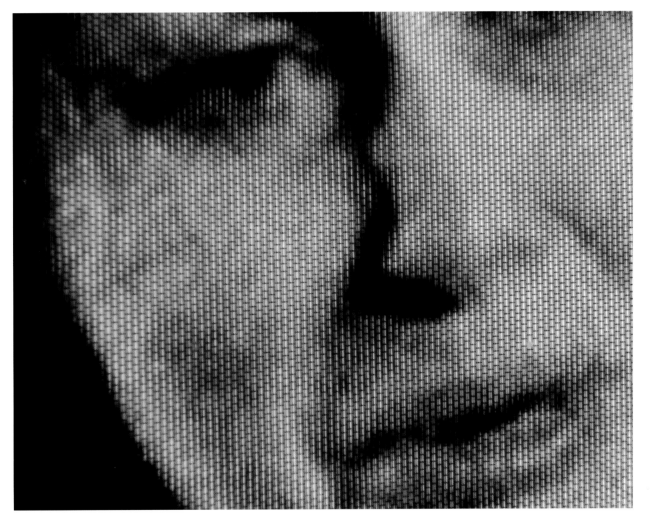

Face

Brendan Derrig

Hallowed Be Their Names

Talking About Planting

Shark - July 2005

St. John's Eve – Maam Valley

Once A Man

The Field And I

Letter From Prison

Iarla Mongey

Hallowed Be Their Names

I know that Belarus is not Russia.
You told me.
But you are the closest person
to Russia, I know.
This is about the children.
It's all I can do.
Did you know
love
travels faster
than light.

Michael J Smyth

Talking About Planting

Cadmus planted teeth
From which brave warriors bloomed.
Me, I plant nothing
Only prune.
Each budding thought,
Harrow it thin
Scrape inside the kernel
Before the flower begins.

Geraldine Mitchell

Shark - July 2005
(i.m. Jean Charles de Menezes)

As I walked west from Dooniver Strand
Slievemore broke through the bog
Thrusting up through black butter
Scattering sundew asphodel and heather
With its glistening fin

And I thought of a Brazilian kitchen
When the worst news burst
Through the flat sea of poverty
Policemen's peaked caps exploding
Through the white-washed walls
Destroying in an instant
A threadbare couple's present
Their future and their past

St. John's Eve – Maam Valley

I am a speck and the page is vast
The darkening hills wide-angle out
And deep ahead layer after layer
Arrange themselves in elegant pleats
Green and green and then almost black

St John's Eve – half past ten –
In that place between dog and wolf
Where light fades invisibly
Oh so politely retiring with only
The faintest click of the latch
Then is gone

Or is it?
Some clouds at the back
In the gaps towards eternity
Are hugging themselves
Holding on to the memory of sun
Calling the eye on, come on, what are you afraid of?

Away from the rim
Well back from the edge
Unkempt mists
Cling to hilltops
Wrapping the sheep up in shrouds

By my wheel
On the roadside
Midsummer colours
Merge and mix

I am a speck and the page is vast
A giant watercolour
Still wet

Seán Lysaght

Once A Man

The hag saw a naked man very briefly
    in the space between a woodcock's design
    and that of a fidgeting siskin.

She saw his bare, skinny arms
    fitting a ruff's headdress,
    his legs disappear into a merganser.

She heard a bunting in a million rushes,
    counting the stems.
When he faltered on the fourth chirp,
    she knew it was him.

She remembered how he gargled in the bathroom
    when a raven called.

She could trace where he waited
    to rob a mallard
    in a grove of twayblades

by a mayfly
    writhing in a spiderweb
    and the ivy crucified to the trees –

bitter old hag
    limping back to an outhouse
    with the bulk of a dead goose,

ripping him open, stripping his cover,
    busy in the smoke of his down,

to bring out the man in him
    and hang his goose pimples in her pantry.

Ndrek Gjini

3. The Field And I

The field and I had cut our hair
last afternoon.
We had a shower by rain
last night.

Today, the field was woken up
by a kiss of the rainbow.
Me, by my mother's phone-call

4. Letter From Prison

My dear friend!
This letter for you
I've written down
here in this green jail
where my word smells like grass.
And my dreams are getting wet in the rain.

Here, where the life and death
have no demarcation line.

Here, where the grass, the rain and flowers
are giving up the ghost
and being born again into a day
as if by magic.

Tanker

Directions

Decisive Moments

Abstract I & II

Famine Ridges, Blacksod

Morning Dew, Moore Hall

Hand Cut Turf

Chrysalis I & II

Tanker

Tracy Sweeney

Directions

Tracy Sweeney

Tracy Sweeney

Abstract I

Mark F Chaddock

Abstract II

Mark F Chaddock

Famine Ridges, Blacksod

Rosalind Davies

Morning Dew, Moore Hall

Leo Fitzgerald

Hand Cut Turf

Rosalind Davies

Caroline Hopkins

Chrysalis I

Chrysalis II

Caroline Hopkins

The Slugs Of Minaun

Song

A Ritual Of Men

Bríd The Shanachie's Daughter

An Portach

Scréach

Paul Durcan

The Slugs Of Minaun

> *The mindful God abhors untimely growth*
> *- Holderlin*

If I also am to die of cancer of the colon
Let me my last days eke in a room
By the sea with the window open;
A hipflask of morphine;
A warm woman
For a boon companion;
On grey, peach evenings
To be able to go for a crawl
Under the cliffs;
To behold the slugs of Minaun;
The black, black slugs of Minaun.

If I cannot leg it to the cliffs
Let me motor to the cliffs
In my wine-red Opel Astra
Like the Queen of France
In a humble tumbril;
Appeal that my wheels
Not liquidate these creatures
With whom I trumpet an affinity -
A weakness for slow growth;
The slugs of Minaun;
The black, black slugs of Minaun.

Death is a puck-goat -
A blur of bog-cotton on the cliffs;
Let him charge me this way and that,
I'll slip his advances to the last;
Instead, lie down with my slugs;
Dodge his horns and
Curl up sluggish with my slugs;
Drowse with the souls of my slugs;
Staunch, sober, sonorous slugs;
The slugs of Minaun;
The black, black slugs of Minaun.

Michelle O'Sullivan

Song

Can you sing them
She asked
The salmon, a woman.
How d'ya mean
He said
The traveller, a man.
Read it and you will hear it
He thinks.
Listen and you will dance
She muses.
Cara m'anam.

Geraldine Cummins

A Ritual Of Men

Height matching height
bearing the burden of death.
Does the mind go blank?
Does it hurt the shoulder
more than the heart?
Is it different each time?
Who decides who's too short
or even who's too tall?
What signals time to change
to another matching set?
Is it ever deemed too far,
too much, too heavy?
Does relief outweigh sadness
when the empty ground is reached
and the whiskey-numbed digging complete?

While the women cut the ham, the bread
and make the tea.

Steve Dunford

Bríd The Shanachie's Daughter

Last night a white and fragile frost clung like lace to the windows of old Killala
And down by Lacken just for an instant the gulls rose high above the bay in a
reverential revolt
A November moon beamed bright haloes on a Foghill tide
And in this epiphany the seaweed shone

At dawn as the last sea salted wind breathed a lull
I awoke from a black heart dream
And on the breeze fond hushed words told me what I already knew

The tide is full in now and the back strands all white with waves and spurts of spray
That sturdy old Atlantic sun has finally set West on a magical place
A storied place where as a child in the height of contentment you dabbled bare feet in
transparent pools
And paddled with Mac Ruairí under the shadows of ancient rocks

Early this morning beneath the picture of the Sacred Heart your lifelong votive lamp
quietly quenched
And as the last sparks of ash cast an immortal light on your always welcoming hearth
Your spirited eyes which once gazed on rebels
emptied of everything but peace

Cast off Bríd
Pull hard on the oars and make for home

Pádhraic Ó Láimhín

An Portach

Is fuath liom an portach
Scaradh is gróigiú móna
A brúscar agus púdar
Im' shúile, béal is scórnach.

Cuileoga is míoltóga
Ionsaíoch faoi theas
Scealpóga is liomóga
Á dhingiú i mo chneas.

Fóid slíocach sleamhnach
Ag boilsciú trí mo lámha
Is fraoch géagach gairgeach
Ag scríobadh feol mo chnámha.

Stuaic im' dhroim ón gcromadh
Strompadh ar gach alt
M' artairi á chalcadh
Ó aontonacht mo thaisc.

Is gráin liom na poill criathraigh
Dubh-uiscí na mboladh mbréan
B'fhearr liom sciúirsiú Chríosta
Ná portach faoi mo dhéin.

Scréach

Im' luí ar ardán aille
Ar airde úire aeir.
Sáile im'intinn
Olagón im' spéir

Faoileáin faiteach fiagach
Ag éagnú dromchla mara
Análú domhain farraige
Tré chlasáin clocha caladh.

Ach is fuar mo leacán aille
A nimhníonn fuil is féith
Mar i bhfíochracht anfach mara
Do chailleas grá mo chléibh.

I ndoimhneachtaí m'fharraige
Tá dubhluachar mo bhrón
Is chuig imeallacht mo spéartha
Scréachaim m'olagóin.

Keem Strand, Achill

Jewel In The Rushes

Daisy Admirer

Rock

Doolough

Mushroom I   Mushroom II

Lydia And Meg   The Trees

Keem Strand, Achill

James Wright

Kevin Murphy

Daisy Admirer

Kevin Murphy

Rock

Paul Kinsella

Doolough

Paul Kinsella

Mushroom I

Christine Reilly

Christine Reilly

Rosalind
Davies

Trish Forde

Dhá Bharra De Nóta fada

The Musicmaker **Horses**

Road Rabbit

Art Ó Súilleabháin

Dhá Bharra De Nóta Fada
(ag faire ar mo Dhaid ag múineadh a phoirt ag m'iníon Aoibhinm)

Ó na méaracha scealptha
dá lámha snáitheacha,
munglaíonn feadóg stadach.

Bogann a rithim maolaithe
céimeanna corracha a chuid faillí,
stracann mionbhuillí a chos le cuimhne.

Ach titeann nótaí fada fonnmhara óna shásamh suaimhneach.

Leanann sise a mhéarchéimeanna tuatacha
trí mhaisiú gléasach na nGarranta Sailí,
i gciúnas leata ar an bhfoghlaim.

Promhann a súile óga tríd a chuidse
a cheartúcháin i bportaireacht an Chúilfhionn,
maoin stóráilte slán anois ina ndíséad stuama.

Agus corraíonn an ceol caol clannach chuig fonn ríleach na nglún.

Ann Joyce

The Musicmaker

He digs at the mouth of memories,
thumps stories into shape
to suit his humour, speaks them
to no-one in particular.

Days, he walks this winter land, searches
for a time that will carry him
trembling to that place, that quick of earth
anointing his working boots.

In his farmer's clothes, his hands
guide the single plough, open drills
in the earth, a stray tune lingers
on the lip of a field.

Clay moves in the grass. The horse
walks straight bars of notes,
his head dips, rises, shakes the unsteady bit
in the forward leap of a turning tune.

In this field he plays a lament to love.
Time enters the door to his bones,
the scent of earth and the scent of woman
at the tips of his fingers.

He wanted to ground her, fine-tune her
to his own beat but she was a symphony,
movements of a melody that differed
from the airs that grew out of this landscape –

hoof-prints in ploughed furrows,
loose stones fallen from a limestone wall,
whitethorn hedges, reddening
a November day, fierce as a single note.

Horses

Summer came with difficulty
like a woman in long labour.
Withered needles of cypress trees
hold their position
fulfil their duty as wind-break.

There is no escape in this landscape,
everything understands its role.
Ghostly shapes of hawthorn
keep fields apart and in the spaces
between, grass weaves,
rolls toward the sea in waves.

Teach me to remember these spaces
and the two chestnut horses
feeding from the same table,
their bodies touching,
neck and nose close
as young love whispering together.

On this ledge at the edge
of the sea, in this July
in Mayo, teach me
to remember the tossing mane,
the heat of the flesh,
the green sea.

Tomás Lally

Road Rabbit

Legs stretched and flopped young head
  Extended on a white line pillow,
    Magpies arc: two for joy
Ready for a pecking frenzy.

Red Door   Sad Suitcase

Fisheye

Hands

John F. Kennedy

Techno   *Diesel Tank*

Tractor In The Rain

Washing Day

John Corless

Sad Suitcase

Aisling Flynn

Fisheye

Aisling Flynn

Hands

Conor Mc Keown

John F. Kennedy

Paul Tarpey

Techno

Paul Tarpey

Diesel Tank

Paul Tarpey

Glenda Colquhoun

Glenda Colquhoun

153

Eire   For Jeannie   Separation

Gary Leahy

Separation

I was gathering up the coal bags
That we'd stuffed behind the oil tank.
We were packing up our goods,
Clearing out the house,
And going our separate ways.
Several years of coal bags,
So much coal we burnt!
All those fires we sat beside
Basking in the warmth.
Cosy winter nights talking, loving,
Reading, playing cards,
Drinking wine, sipping gin,
Feet propped against the fireplace,
Warm bodied, warm hearts.

All those fires, ashes now;
Smoky memories
That sting my eyes to tears.

Cleo Watson

For Jeannie

Leaving bed pans (the metal type) behind us
   we trucked it to London courtesy of Alf.
     London Bridge just after dawn
   we were invincible with jeans and pony-tails.
Sixties Soho decadence with espresso everywhere
   a café called Le Macabre so avant-garde then
     but dull and passé in the new millennium.
   We had the eyes of children and watched with delight
as bowler hats and rolled umbrellas crossed the Thames.
   In Cornwall with a fleeting notion of the Scilly Isles
     but our time was running out.
I still think about that tomato boat we left behind.

Jacek Kozik

Eire

Witasz mnie Irlandio swoim surowym krajobrazem gdzie
wichry roznoszą po kamienistych polach skargi twych dalekich przodków i widzę jak
w Temple Bar Wikingowie handlują ludźmi niczym dzisiejsi farmerzy na targu
owcami

Przemierzyłem cię aż po wyspy Aran do których
kołysany morzem zawitałem zeszłej jesieni by uczyć się
szeptu setek kamiennych ogrodów gdzie od zawsze nie rosną drzewa a
martwe resztki ścian opuszczonych kościołów powoli
nasyca wilgoć oceanu

Jak dzisiaj pamiętam twe klify mierzące się z potęgą Atlantyku
broniące dostępu do twych włości swym bazaltowym przepychem

Stanąłem na twym brzegu by
zostać pokonanym przez nostalgię wiszącą w powietrzu i by
na Sally Gap pośród purpury wrzosów leczyć umęczone serce

Eire

Eire/you welcome me with your rugged landscape/where the winds carry the
complaints of your ancestors over the stony fields/and where in Temple Bar the
Vikings sell people just as today's farmers sell sheep at the market

I have traveled as far as the Aran Islands where/rocked by the sea I came last autumn
to learn/the whispers of hundreds of stony gardens where trees never grew/and the
dead remains of abandoned churches slowly/soak in the humidity of the ocean

I still remember your cliffs measuring up to the might of the Atlantic/protecting your
relams with their basalt splendour

I stopped on your shore/to be defeated by the nostalgia hanging in the air/to heal
the tired heart among the purple heaths of Sally Gap/to be overwhelmed by the steep

zostać przygwożdżonym przez wbite stromo w ziemię góry skrywające
u podnóża metalową czerń jeziora kojącą rany pięćdziesięcioletnich oczu

Ruszyłem też na północ by
zobaczyć twoje zbuntowane włości oraz groblę tego olbrzyma który
nigdy nie doszedł do majaczącej za morzem Szkocji a znaczy to że
wybrał ciebie

Wyznam ci Irlandio: uciekałem przed światem już niejednokrotnie
kryjąc się po różnych miastach Europy
od przepychu Monte Carlo po zgnuśniałą sytość Amsterdamu
w pokojach pełnych książek szukałem ukojenia i w niezliczonych rozmowach
szermowałem słowem nie wiedząc że nadaremno gdyż
niósł mnie przywilej młodości: wiara w to co mówię

Aż dopadł mnie tu
na krańcach Europy i swoim przepychem powalił na kolana
księżycowy krajobraz wzgórz za Letterkenny które
co wieczór znaczą słoneczną krwią swe zbocza i stanąłem jak wryty
na Horn Head nie wiedząc co począć – porażony pięknem

mountains/hiding the metalic blackness of a lake at their feet/to heal the wounds of
fifty-year-old eyes

I also traveled to the North/to see your rebelious villages and the causeway of that
giant/who never made it to Scotland beyond the sea/which means that he chose you

I confess to you, Ireland, many a time I have run away from the world/hiding in
different cities of Europe/from the splendour of Monte Carlo to the decadent
prosperity of Amsterdam/in rooms full of books I sought peace of mind and in
numerous conversations/I fought with words as weapons not knowing how futile the
struggle was/for I was guided by the privilege of youth: conviction in what I say

Until the lunar landscape of the hills of Letterkenny found me here at the end of Europe
/and brought me down on my knees with its splendour/the slopes covered with the
blood of the sun every evening/I was fixed to the spot on Horn Head/stunned by its
beauty not knowing what to do

Także twoje południe – gdzie pewnego razu przybiły brygandyny Hiszpanów by
zdradzić twoje dzieci i pozostawić ślad swojej bytności w potomkach tamtych kobiet
– było łaskawe memu sercu gdyż przemierzając przylądki mogłem zanurzyć się
w świat tak daleki że niewyrażalny inaczej niż
przez łzę co do której nigdy nie podejrzewałem iż
może się pojawić

O Eire Eire czy jesteś mi łaskawa?
Tego nie odgadnę gdyż wędrowanie stało się przywilejem nieszczęśliwych więc
błąkam się w tym tłumie szukając swojego kamienia filozoficznego niczym
Krainy Wiecznej Młodości do której podobno
niedaleko z twoich rubieży

Wybacz mi Irlandio że zdradzę cię jak każde inne miejsce na tej ziemi i już niedługo
znowu wyruszę lecz obiecuję że w sercu wezmę cię ze sobą
i tak już zostanie po
ostatni oddech oznajmiający przegraną do której
nie będę miał żalu jak
mieć nigdy nie można do czegoś co
jest nieuchronne

Also your South, where the Spanish brigands arrived once to betray your children/
and leave a trace of their presence in the descendants of those women,/was
favourable to me, for travelling across the cape I could immerse myself in the world
so remote/it was inexpressible except through a tear/which I never suspected I
could shed

Oh Eire, Eire, are you favourable to me?/I will never know that because travelling
has become a priviledge of the unhappy/and I feel lost in the crowd looking for my
philosopher's stone/like the Land of Eternal Youth which they say is not far from
your shores

Forgive me, Ireland, if I betray you like any other place on earth/and before long I
will depart again but I promise to take you with me in my heart/and so it will remain
until the last breath that announces the failure/which I will not regret/for one cannot
regret what is inevitable

Biographical Notes

Poets

Heinrich Böll (pp.1-3): Nobel Prize for Literature 1972. Travelled from Germany to Achill with his family in the 1950s, spent regular and extended periods of time there in the following two decades.

Kevin Bowen (pp.11-12): poet, translator, and director of the William Joiner Center for the Study of War and Social Consequences, University of Massachusetts, Boston. Spends part of each year on Achill Island. Most recent book, *Eight True Maps of the West*, Dedalus 2004.

Mark F Chaddock (pp.63-64): immigrated to Achill Island in 1995 to pursue his love of writing and photography. He is a member of Achill Creative Writers' Group.

Bríd Conroy (p.45): born in Dublin, now living in Mayo. "Words give life to an unspoken part of me. Love it".

John Corless (p.41): writes short stories, drama and "a few poems". He is a founder member of the Claremorris-based Mayo Writers Block.

Geraldine Cummins (p.122): Crann poet 1997 – 2004, Heritage specialist for Heritage in Schools Scheme. She has written and directed several plays for children.

John F Deane (pp.59-61): born Achill Island, founder of Poetry Ireland; latest collection *The Instruments of Art*, Carcanet 2005.

Stephen Dunford (p.123): native of Castlebar: writer, illustrator, musician, historian, currently engaged on four books: covering *The Mayo Táin* to General Humbert.

Paul Durcan (pp.119-120): current Ireland Professor of Poetry at Queens University, Trinity College Dublin, and University College Dublin. Most recent book, *The Art of Life*, The Harvill Press 2004.

Anna Galt (pp.1-3): graduated in English and German from Trinity College Dublin, and recently completed an MPhil in Literary Translation there.

Ndrek Gjini (pp.104-105): Albanian journalist and writer living in Castlebar. Has been writing for *The Connaught Telegraph*. Studied literature in University in Albania, now studying Heritage in G.M.I.T. Castlebar.

Lizann Gorman (p.17): a struggling poet, has spent her entire life in the west. Her work has appeared in other Mayo Anthologies.

Daniel Hickey (pp.88-89): was born in 1980. From Ballina, he has lived in Dublin and Galway. Respects and admires Patrick Kavanagh, for his fantastic, ragged language and his disgust with snobbery.

Ann Joyce (pp.140-142): lived in Turlough before moving to Co. Sligo. A poetry chapbook, *Threads from Maeve's Mantle*. Her poetry collection, *Watching for Signs*, Dedalus 2005.

Ursula Kelly (pp.68-69): a founder member of Ballycastle Writer's Group, loves to capture significant moments in free style poetry.

Jacek Kozik (pp.157-159): born 1955 in Katowice. Graduated from the Department of Philosophy and Sociology at the University of Warsaw. Zbigniew Herbert has described his poems as "a rare example of finding one's own voice in poetry".

Teresa Lally (pp.85-87): from Tourmakeady, Co. Mayo. Living in Dublin. Work published in *Cyphers*, *Force 10*, *Poetry Ireland Review*, and other publications.

Tomás Lally (p.143): lives in Partry, Co. Mayo. He would like to be a published poet and novelist when he grows up, or beforehand if possible!

Gary Leahy (p.155): grew up in West Cork and now lives in Newport, where he works as a maker of violin-bows.

Una Leavy (p.15): born in and living near Charlestown. "Attempting to write poetry all my life."

Sabra Loomis (pp.66-67): divides her time between New York and Achill, most recent book, *Rose Tree*, (Alice James Books). Published in *Cyphers*, *Poetry Ireland Review*, etc.

Seán Lysaght (pp.13-14, 103): was born in 1957 and grew up in Limerick. Four collections of poems, and a biography, *Robert Lloyd Praeger: The Life of a Naturalist*. He teaches at the Galway-Mayo Institute of Technology, Castlebar.

Maureen Maguire (p.46): evacuated from Coventry and brought up by her grandparents in Cregganbawn, Louisburgh, then lived in England for over fifty years. This is her first poem in print.

Benny Martin (p.47): born and bred in Castlebar. Taught in Burren and Derrywash schools. Married to Marion, with four children.

Jo McCormick Phillips (p.65): is living in England at the moment, but having just spent ten years in Mayo considers herself a Mayo poet.

Terry McDonagh (pp.25-26): poet, dramatist and teacher, returned to his native Mayo, (Killedan), after over twenty years in Germany. Four books of poetry, a book of letters and a short novel for children.

Peggy McGing (p.83): born and raised in Letterbrock, Westport. Currently studying radio production. She is interested in all aspects of creative writing.

Geraldine Mitchell (pp.101-102): a member of Louisburgh Writers' Group, she has written two novels for children and a biography, as well as poetry. She moved to Killeen in 2000.

Iarla Mongey (p.99): published in Mayo Anthologies, co-edited *Years Of Mondays*. Read at Cúirt, The Irish Writers' Centre, Westport Arts. Stayed in the Böll Cottage, Achill.

Colette Nic Aodha (pp.27-28, 62): born Shrule, Co. Mayo. Poetry collections *Baill Seirce*; *Faoi Chrann Cnó Capaill*; *Gallúnach-Ar-Rópa*, and, (in English), *Sundial*. Short stories: *Ádh Mór*.

Pádhraic Ó Láimhín (pp.124-125): rugadh é i gCeathrú Mór-Leacain agus tá sé fós ina chónaí sa bparóiste inar rugadh é. Is múinteoir bunscoile é agus é ina chó-ordnaitheoir ag freastal ar cheithre scoil sa cheantar.

Art Ó Súilleabháin (p.139): rugadh agus tógadh é i gContae na Gaillimhe ach cónaíonn sé anois i gCeathrú na gCon i gContae Mhaigh Eo. Tá filíocht i mBéarla agus i nGaeilge foilsithe aige, agus leabhar staire, *Ages Ago*.

Michelle O' Sullivan (p.121): has a BA and MA in Literature. She lives along the Moy, between Ballina and Enniscrone.

Bríd Quinn (p.16): likes to make people laugh, and think. Member of Castlebar Writers' Group, which, like poetry, is a refuge, an inspiration and really good fun.

Ger Reidy (pp. 81-82): *Pictures from a Reservation*, Dedalus 1998. Three more collections completed. Widely published, has received various national poetry awards, and an Arts Council Bursary.

Mary Catherine Reilly (p.84): graduated from UCG in 1989, with a degree in English Literature and Philosophy. Since then she has been travelling, teaching, and – more recently – writing poetry.

Ewa Sadowska: (pp.157-159): MPhil graduate in English from the University of Warsaw, and MLitt in Early Irish Literature from Trinity College Dublin, currently working on a project on iconicity in Old Irish.

Michael J Smyth (p.100): from Straide Co. Mayo. He is projects co-ordinator with Mayo Artsquad, community arts group.

Jean Tuomey (p.29): grew up in Dundalk and lives in Castlebar. A former teacher, she now facilitates Creative Writing classes.

Caitríona Uí Oistín (pp.42-43): as Tír Eoghain. Lonnaithe i gCathair na Mart le roinnt blianta. Ag obair sa G.M.I.T. Caisleán an Bharraigh.

Cleo Watson (p.156): was published in the *White Seahorse Anthology*, won the Midwest Radio Award for Poetry in 1997. Her latest collection is called *On The Swing Of Memory*.

Mary Whelan (p.44): lives at Treenbeg, near Newport. She is a member of Louisburgh Writers' Group.

Photographers

Michael Blake (pp.32-35): is a photographic artist, based in Connemara.

Mark F Chaddock (pp.110-111): is a visual artist and writer living on Achill Island.

John Corless (p.145): mainly photographs buildings, seeking to convey the experience of being in and around a constructed environment.

Glenda Colquhoun (p152-153): has had a lifelong passion for photography. She is a professional photographer and lecturer living in Achill.

Michael Conlon (pp.92-93): is a professional photographer and artist from Pontoon. He is now based in Dublin.

Rosalind Davies (pp.112-113, 115, 136): lives in Newport. She has worked at various times as a photographer, a college lecturer, and an artist.

Brendan Derrig (pp. 96-97): is an artist who has just graduated with a BA Honours in Fine Art and is currently based in Galway.

Leo Fitzgerald (p.114): lives in Castlebar. He took up photography seriously in 2005. His favourite subjects are landscape, architecture and people.

Aisling Flynn (pp.146-147): earned her Fine Art degree from G.M.I.T., Galway in 2002. She now lives in Co. Mayo where photography forms an integral part of her artistic practice.

Trish Forde (p.137): is a photographer and is based in Ballinrobe.

Paul Fullard (pp.50-51): has a degree in Fine Art from G.M.I.T. Now living in Dublin, he works through the medium of photography with digital processing.

Michael Gannon (p.5): is a member of the Castlebar Camera Club. He lives in Liscarney, Westport.

Andrew Hebden (pp.54-55, 74-75): is a documentary photographer.

Keith Heneghan (pp.19, 23): is a press photographer based in Castlebar, Co. Mayo.

Caroline Hopkins (pp.116-117): is a multi-media installation artist. She has recently returned from China and is currently based in Co. Mayo.

Noreen Hopkins (pp.94-95): has a degree in Photography (Hons) from the University of Wales, Newport. She is currently living and working in Galway.

Paul Kinsella (pp.130-133): is a professional photographer, originally from Dublin, now living and working in Claremorris, Co. Mayo.

Conor McKeown (pp.76-77, 148): gained a BA(Hons) in Photography from Trent University in 1999. He lives in Westport and works throughout the west.

Michael McLaughlin (pp.20-21, 71-73): is a professional photographer from Westport. He specialises in photojournalism and landscape.

Margo McNulty (pp.36-37): is an artist. She was born on Achill Island and now lives and works in the midlands.

Kevin Murphy (pp128-129): is an amateur photographer based in Westport, who specialises in photographing local wildlife.

Art Ó Súilleabháin (p.9): is writer, artist, teacher and father from Carnacon.

Jan Pesch (pp.49, 52-53): is a framer and aerial photographer originally from Hamburg, Germany. He runs a photographic gallery in Westport.

Dobromir Petrov (pp.6-7, 57): is an amateur photographer who works as a hair stylist. He prefers to work in black and white.

Thomas Reaney (p.8): is a photographer living in Co. Mayo. His photographs record his vision of the County's people and its landscape.

Christine Reilly (pp.134-135): is a keen amateur photographer. She enjoys photographing nature and people.

Olivia Smyth (pp.38-39): is an amateur photographer from Claremorris.

Tracy Sweeney (pp.107-109): is a printmaker and photographer from Castlebar. Her work is concerned with issues of location and placement. She utilises digital media and traditional print making processes.

Paul Tarpey (pp.56, 149-151): is a photographer based in Limerick. He is currently exploring issues surrounding landscape, using both video and still images.

Graham Temple (pp.31, 78-79): is an amateur photographer living in Louisburgh, Co. Mayo.

Francis Van Maele (p.91): lives in Achill where he makes artist's books in limited editions, using photography, collage and silkscreen printing.

James Wright (p.127): is a semi-professional photographer based in Castlebar. He works under the trade name 'Studio 094'.